Your Senses

by Helen Frost

Consulting Editor: Gail Saunders-Smith, Ph.D.

Consultant: Eric H. Chudler, Ph.D.
Research Associate Professor
Department of Anesthesiology
University of Washington, Seattle

Pebble Books

an imprint of Capstone Press
Mankato, Minnesota

Pebble Books are published by Capstone Press
818 North Willow Street, Mankato, Minnesota 56001
http://www.capstone-press.com

Library of Congress Cataloging-in-Publication Data
Frost, Helen, 1949–
    Your senses/by Helen Frost.
    p. cm.—(The senses)
    Includes bibliographical references and index.
    Summary: Simple text and photographs present the five senses and how they
work together.
    ISBN 0-7368-0387-4
    1. Senses and sensation—Juvenile literature. [1. Senses and sensation.] I. Title.
II. Series: Frost, Helen, 1949– The senses.
QP434.F76   2000
612.8—dc21   99-18966
                                                                                    CIP

Note to Parents and Teachers

The Senses series supports national science standards for units
related to behavioral science. This book describes and illustrates
the five senses. The photographs support early readers in
understanding the text. The repetition of words and phrases
helps early readers learn new words. This book also introduces
early readers to subject-specific vocabulary words, which are
defined in the Words to Know section. Early readers may need
assistance to read some words and to use the Table of Contents,
Words to Know, Read More, Internet Sites, and Index/Word
List sections of the book.

Table of Contents

You have five senses.
Your senses let you
see, hear, smell,
taste, and touch.

eye

nose

ear

tongue

skin

Your eyes, ears, nose, tongue, and skin have sensors. The sensors send signals to your brain.

Your brain understands the signals. The signals tell you about everything around you.

You see with your eyes. You see shapes, sizes, and colors.

You hear with your ears. You hear high sounds and low sounds. You hear soft sounds and loud sounds.

You smell with your nose. You like some smells. You do not like other smells.

You taste with your tongue. You taste sweet foods and sour foods. You taste bitter foods and salty foods.

18

You touch with your skin. You touch hot things and cold things. You touch soft things and hard things.

Your senses work together.
They help you understand
what is around you.

Words to Know

bitter—a strong and unsweet taste; orange peels taste bitter.

brain—the body part inside your head that controls your body; your brain understands the signals that your senses send.

detect—to notice something; your sensors detect things about your surroundings.

nerve—a bundle of thin fibers that sends signals between your brain and other parts of your body

sense—a way of knowing about things around you; hearing, seeing, smelling, tasting, and touching are your five senses.

sensor—a cell that detects things around you; sensors send signals to your brain.

signal—a message; signals travel along nerves to your brain.

sour—a strong, acid taste; lemons taste sour.

Read More

Bennett, Paul. *My Brain and Senses.* Bodyworks. Parsippany, N.J.: Silver Press, 1998.

Maurer, Tracy. *The Senses.* Bodyworks. Vero Beach, Fla.: Rourke, 1999.

Parker, Steve. *Senses.* Look at Your Body. Brookfield, Conn.: Copper Beech Books, 1997.

Tatchell, Judy. *How Do Your Senses Work?* Flip Flaps. London: Usborne Publishing, 1997.

Internet Sites

Come to Your Senses
http://tqjunior.advanced.org/3750

The Senses
http://faculty.washington.edu/chudler/chsense.html

Teaching Children about the Five Senses
http://www.urbanext.uiuc.edu/nibbles/succeed-senses.html

Index/Word List

Word Count: 138
Early-Intervention Level: 13

Editorial Credits
Mari C. Schuh, editor; Timothy Halldin, cover designer; Kimberly Danger,
   photo researcher

Photo Credits
Bill Losh/FPG International LLC, cover
David F. Clobes, 4 (bottom right), 6, 18
Index Stock Imagery, 4 (top right), 8
Photo Network/Tom McCarthy, 4 (top left); Myrleen Cate, 4 (bottom left), 10, 12
Unicorn Stock Photos/Martha McBride, 16
Uniphoto, 1, 20
Visuals Unlimited/Bill Beatty, 4 (center); Dick Thomas, 14